# LET'S CELEB

## DESIGN AND TECHNOLOGY
## *interactions*
### STARTING POINT

## THE DESIGN DIMENSION EDUCATIONAL TRUST

PROJECT CONSULTANT
Tristram Shepard

Stanley Thornes (Publishers) Ltd

Text © Design Dimension Educational Trust (Chris Whitehead, Anita Cormac, Roger Standen) 1991

Original artwork by Mark Miller
© Stanley Thornes (Publishers) Ltd 1991

All rights reserved. No part of this publication may be reproduced or transmitted in any form or by any means, electronic or mechanical, including photocopy, recording or any information storage and retrieval system, without permission in writing from the publisher or under licence from the Copyright Licensing Agency Limited. Further details of such licences (for reprographic reproduction) may be obtained from the Copyright Licensing Agency Limited, of 90 Tottenham Court Road, London W1P 9HE.

First published in 1991 by:
Stanley Thornes (Publishers) Ltd
Old Station Drive
Leckhampton
CHELTENHAM   GL53 0DN
England

**British Library Cataloguing in Publication Data**
 Standen, Roger
  Let's celebrate.
  I. Title   II. Cormac, Anita
  III. Whitehead, Chris
  394.2
  ISBN 0-7487-1162-7

Typeset by Florencetype Ltd, Kewstoke, Avon

Printed and bound by the Times Printing Group, Singapore

# Contents

|  | page |
|---|---|
| **Introduction** | 2 |
| **Thinking about Places** | 4 |
| **Thinking about Food** | 6 |
| **Thinking about Dressing up** | 8 |
| **Thinking about Organisation** | 10 |
| **Birthdays** | 12 |
| **Commemoration** | 16 |
| **Carnivals** | 20 |
| **Festivals** | 24 |
| **Events** | 28 |
| *Acknowledgements* | 30 |

# INTRODUCTION

## Thinking about celebrating something? Thinking about how to celebrate it?

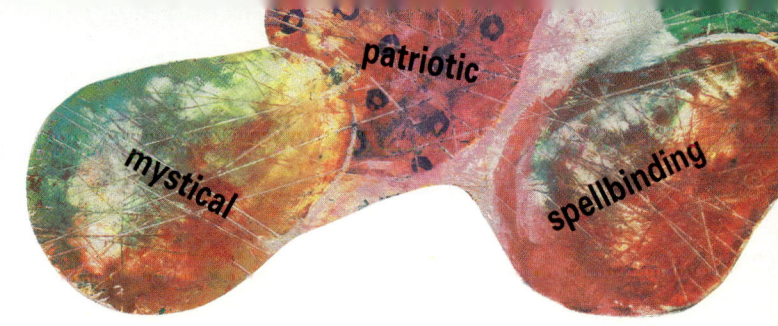

*mystical*  *patriotic*  *spellbinding*

**This book is about celebrations:** what they are, and how we celebrate. When we celebrate we do something special to show that a day or an event is important. While some celebrations are quiet, personal occasions which happen at home, others are noisy, public, and involve large numbers of people. Whatever the scale of the celebration however, planning is important. This book will give you some ideas for your projects on celebrations and festivals.

Some celebrations are centred around commemorations, rituals and ceremonies, and others, such as Christmas, are based on religious beliefs. These traditional celebrations may be difficult to change. You may be able to think of some other celebrations which always remain the same simply because no one has considered changing them. Why not suggest an alternative?

SPECIAL EFFECTS

Some celebrations, such as birthday parties, can provide enormous scope for original ideas. Let your imagination run away with you! You might be able to think of some completely new kinds of celebration. You might want to recognise someone's good work: a composer, architect, inventor, artist or someone who has worked hard for charity. You might want to celebrate something in nature: a season, or a planet, for example. What would you do for a celebration of friendship? Would you make presents, send greetings, create a carnival? Think about creating a celebration based on a nursery rhyme character. Perhaps you could organise an event for young children or you might enact the nursery rhyme story. Such original celebrations can involve the invention of new rituals and ceremonies and the creation of new products.

MUSIC

DANCING

Other celebrations are linked to the preservation of the past: like veteran car runs, air displays, traction engine rallies and special exhibitions. In contrast, new things can also be celebrated: the opening of a new shop or building, the launch of a new car, the first night of a drama production.

**Using this book.** What do all celebrations have in common? They are usually associated with places, food, dressing up, and a lot of organisation. These four common elements are presented in the first part of this book. The rest of the book then focuses in turn on particular types of celebration: birthdays, commemorations, carnivals, festivals, and other events. Questions are asked about the sights, sounds, smells and emotions which are unique to celebrations. You can contrast the different celebrations.

HAVING A GOOD TIME

You can use this book as a starting point to prompt your ideas and feelings about celebrations. Let it spark your imagination. What you create is up to you.

*poignant*  *thrilling*  *enjoyable*

stimulating  
religious  
amazing  
magical  
unusual  
moving

**SURPRISES**

**TRADITIONS**

**RITUALS**

**REMEMBERING**

**CEREMONIES**

**EATING**

riveting     spectacular     tear-jerking

# Thinking about PLACES

**What sorts of places are suitable for large, public celebrations?**

- Where would be a good place to hold an exhibition, review or reception?
- Where would be a safe site for a firework display?
- Where would the best viewing points be?
- Would it be a good idea to organise a public concert?
- How would the crowds be organised?

- What public facilities (such as car parks and toilets) are available?
- Will extra facilities need to be provided?
- Where should food and refreshments be situated?
- Where could unusual environments for celebrations be created?

- Where could a procession be assembled?
- What route could a procession take?
- Where would it start and finish?
- Which streets could be decorated?
- Which streets would need to be closed to traffic?

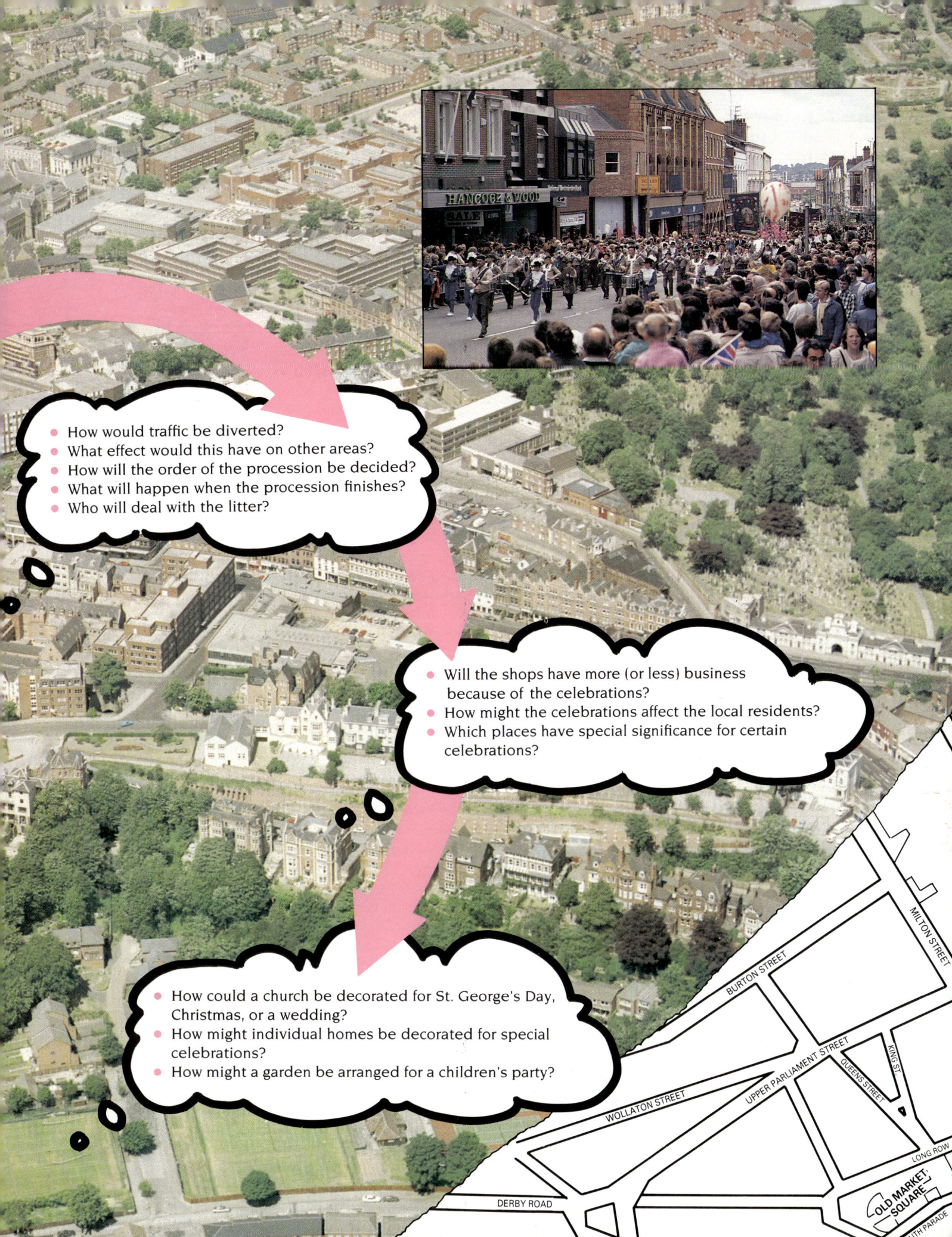

- How would traffic be diverted?
- What effect would this have on other areas?
- How will the order of the procession be decided?
- What will happen when the procession finishes?
- Who will deal with the litter?

- Will the shops have more (or less) business because of the celebrations?
- How might the celebrations affect the local residents?
- Which places have special significance for certain celebrations?

- How could a church be decorated for St. George's Day, Christmas, or a wedding?
- How might individual homes be decorated for special celebrations?
- How might a garden be arranged for a children's party?

# Thinking about FOOD

**Food is an important part of most celebrations. Careful planning is essential whether the occasion is an intimate meal for two, a snack from a stall, or an enormous banquet.**

List the foods you might serve at each of the meals mentioned above.
Ask yourself:

- Where will the celebration take place?
- How many people will need feeding?
- How will the food be eaten?
- What ingredients will you need?
- How much will it all cost to buy?
- Will you make all the dishes or buy some ready-made?
- How long will the food take to prepare?
- Is any special equipment required to prepare the food?
- What kinds of cutlery and serving dishes are needed?
- How will the food be transported?
- How might it be packed?
- What kinds of materials would be suitable?
- Is the food to be sold?
- How much will you charge?

## Festive Food

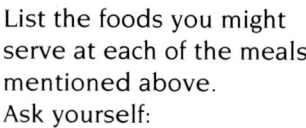

It is easier to calculate quantities of food and materials for small numbers of people. For large numbers however, it is essential to make a careful estimate in advance.

What makes food for celebrations look festive? Here are some suggestions:

- Decorations
- Attractive presentation
- Special table linen and china.

## just this once?

Healthy eating means following some guidelines, such as avoiding foods containing large quantities of white sugar, fats, salt and artificial additives (including colouring). Why is this so? Do some research to find out.

Many of the foods eaten at celebrations are loaded with all of these. Do you think it is important to keep to the guidelines or do you think people should make an exception just this once? What are the alternatives? Think about creating new types of food or presenting familiar food in a new way.

## your catering firm

Imagine you could form a company specialising in providing a complete and out-of-the-ordinary catering service for all kinds of celebrations no matter how bizarre. Begin by discussing the types of celebrations where your services would be valuable. List them for future reference.

What would you be able to offer your clientèle which is unique, attractive and cost effective? It would be useful to find out what existing catering firms are offering. How could you do this? Talk about the things you will need to find out and decisions you will need to make.

- What services can you give?
- Who are the customers likely to be?
- What names and locations are possible?
- What food regulations will you need to follow?
- What do you need to find out about methods of serving the foods?
- How much can you charge?
- How will you transport the food?

You could use this information later, in your company's brochure, for example. What would your company be called? Start by listing some names.

# Thinking about DRESSING UP

Often when people take part in a celebration they need to wear special clothes. There are many practical points to consider.

**Who decides what the costumes** in a celebration should be like? Are they dictated by tradition or is there scope for creating new kinds of clothes?

**Will people need to wear** matching or co-ordinating clothes or costumes? Will the spectators at the celebration need to wear particular types of clothes? How will they choose what to wear? Will the weather matter?

**Will the same colours**, shapes, patterns or textures be used throughout the celebration?

How do you think all the different parts of a costume can be made?

**Think about** hats and headgear, jewellery, make-up, and fabrics. How can these be constructed and manufactured?

**Faces?** Will faces need to be made up in a special way or will masks be worn? Maybe some people do not want to be easily recognised. How can you amuse or frighten people?

**Feet?** Will people need special footwear? Consider the appearance as well as the function.

If you were asked to design an outfit for someone taking part in the school carnival, what factors would you need to consider? Try out some of your ideas using sketches and some materials.

- How might costumes show the theme of celebration?
- How long will they take to make?
- Can existing items of clothing be adapted?
- Will the costumes need to be of different sizes to fit different people?
- How will you arrange the fitting?
- What materials are likely to be suitable?
- What functions will the materials need to serve?
- How durable will the costumes need to be?
- Durability might affect the cost so could the costumes be re-used after the celebration?
- What will happen to the costumes if it is windy or raining?
- Why might people need to practise wearing the costumes?

# Thinking about ORGANISATION

**Big events don't just happen: there is always a lot to consider and manage.**

### Early decisions
- Is there an organising committee?
- What areas of responsibility will there be?
- What background research will be necessary to plan the celebrations?
- How much time is there to organise the celebrations? What important dates will need to be met?

### Events
- What types of activities, entertainments, ceremonies or rituals will take place?
- How will the different activities be connected?
- What will be needed to make them happen?
- Where will the celebrations be held?
- How will the participants know what to do and when to do it?
- Will rehearsals be necessary?

### Publicity
- How will people find out about the celebrations?
- Will there be an advertising campaign?
- What information will people need before and during the celebrations? For example, historical facts, directions, menus, programmes, route maps. Who will produce these?

### Access
- How will people get to the celebration?
- How will people get to and from the events?
- What is the access like?
- Will people need a ticket to the celebrations?
- How much should they cost?

### Facilities
- What facilities will people need? Refreshments? Toilets? Car parks?
- What provisions will be necessary for small children, families, the elderly and the disabled?
- What safety requirements will have to be considered?
- How will people be supervised?
- Will there be crowd control?

### Media
- Who will record the celebrations?
- What arrangements will be made for coverage by the media?

### Budget
- What costs are involved and how will they be met?
- Who is paying for the organisation?
- Who is paying for the advertising campaign?

### Afterwards
- Who will clear up after the celebrations?

# Birthday Celebrations

**Most people celebrate their birthday and arranging a party is one way of making that day special for someone. There are many different ideas and possibilities for planning a birthday celebration.**

**Birthday party food is usually special** and differs from the kind of food eaten every day. What other kinds of food are served in Britain and in other countries for birthday celebrations?

**Balloons, banners, streamers and birthday cards** help to create the party atmosphere. Brightly coloured, shiny or glittery, they can be cheap, disposable, purchased or home made. Think of other imaginative and unusual kinds of decoration suitable for a party. One idea might be to have an Outer Space birthday or some other kind of unusual party. Can you think of any other party themes?

**Planning special birthday surprises** is exciting and challenging. An unexpected present, a funny card or a kissogram are only some of the ways to catch a person unaware. Can you think of others?

**You can get ideas from a great range of birthday cards – from traditional cards to humorous pop-up ones or personalised cards.**

## Things people do

There are many traditional party games, such as musical chairs, pass the parcel, pin the tail on the donkey, blind man's buff, oranges and lemons, musical bumps and charades. Do you know of any other ones?

Why not plan a special outing, perhaps going out for a meal, to the cinema or to the zoo? Some fast food outlets and leisure centres provide special facilities and catering for birthdays.

Discuss the advantages and disadvantages of not celebrating your birthday at home. If you could, where would you choose to go? Have you been on a birthday outing? Did it live up to your expectations?

Planning what to wear is fun. Most people would feel uncomfortable arriving at a party looking out-of-place but whether they are wearing formal or casual clothes, most party-goers like to look different from the way others normally see them.

## Even the best laid plans…

'I spent nearly a year planning a surprise 40th birthday party for my husband. Everyone arrived and we waited and waited. Eventually the telephone rang. It was him. He was at the airport waiting to meet a client – his plane had been delayed six hours. He arrived home at 12.30 p.m. By then everyone had gone home.'

'The day after my birthday party everyone phoned to thank me for inviting them. They all also happened to mention that they had been up for most of the night with an upset stomach. I didn't feel too good myself.'

'I didn't remember putting my brother's birthday cake on the chair until he sat on it.'

'The party for my son seemed to be going well, that is, until the fight started.'

'I was certain that I had confirmed the restaurant reservation for my 25 guests. I expect one day we will look back and laugh about it – the Chinese takeaway really wasn't that bad.'

# BIRTHDAYS

*are about having a...*

dazzling  jolly  happy  frivolous  spectacular  amusing  fun  time

**Good parties need sound planning and organisation.**

**Imagine that you are going to organise** a birthday party for someone you know well. What kinds of things would you need to consider? For example, the age of the person is important; a ninety-five-year-old is unlikely to want to play boisterous party games and a six-year-old may not want to sing old-time music-hall songs around the piano. So knowing who the party is for and the kinds of things they are likely to enjoy are two of the essential factors in birthday party planning. What other aspects do you think you would need to consider?

Of all the people you know, what could you do to make a birthday really special and memorable for one of them?

Could you arrange to:
- Contact old friends?
- Prepare special food?
- Specially decorate a room for a party?
- Dress up in party clothes?
- Organise surprises?
- Go on an outing somewhere special?

If you can, talk to someone who has recently arranged a birthday party. You could find out:

- What factors they had to consider before the party
- The ways other people were able to help
- What costs were involved
- The aspects which worked well and those which did not
- Pitfalls you should avoid.

If you can, talk to someone who has celebrated a birthday recently. You could find out:

- What made it a special day?
- What made it particularly enjoyable?
- Whether they would have altered anything?
- Who arranged the special activities for them?
- Was it recorded in any way for example with photographs or video?
- How would they like to spend their next birthday?

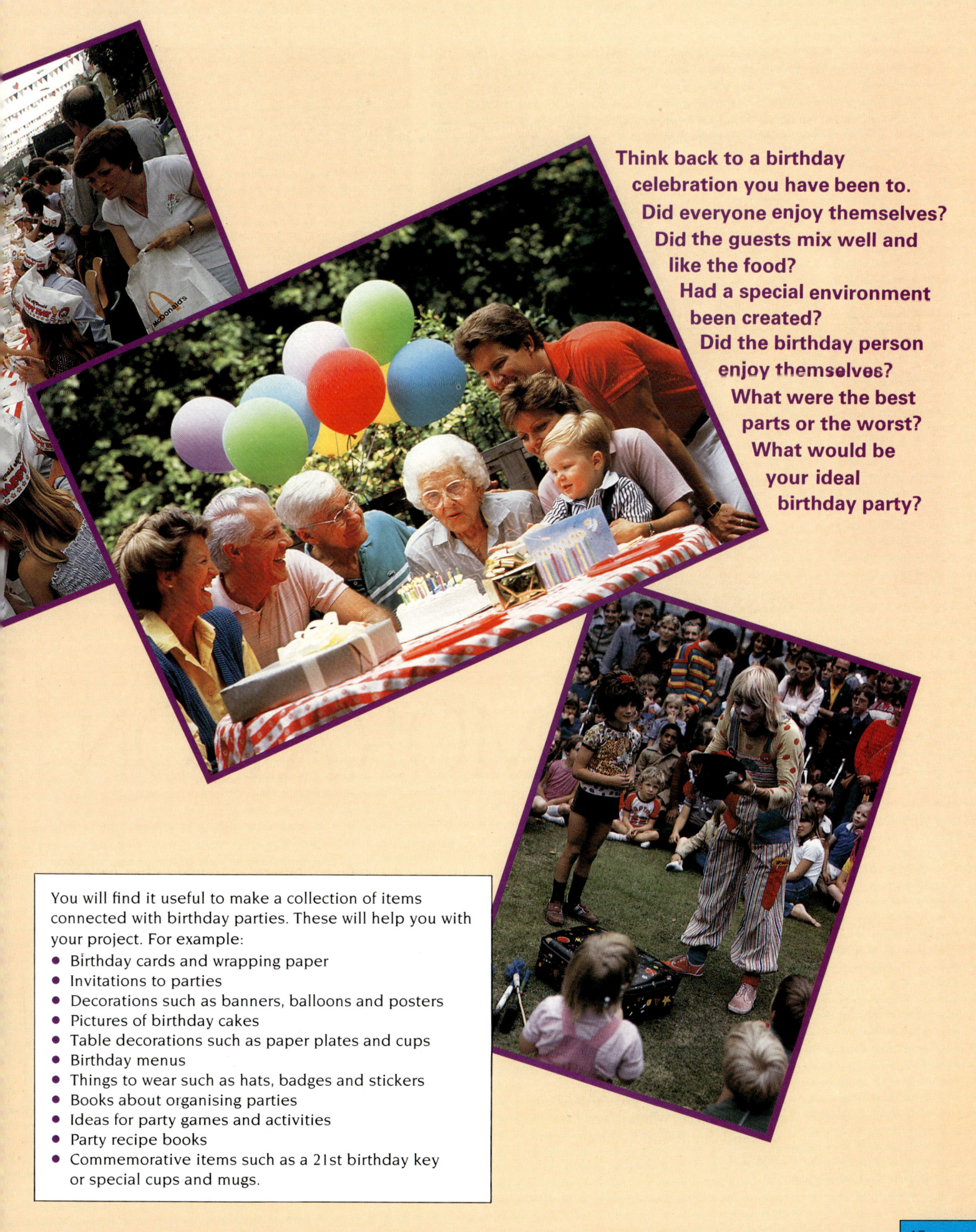

Think back to a birthday celebration you have been to.
Did everyone enjoy themselves?
Did the guests mix well and like the food?
Had a special environment been created?
Did the birthday person enjoy themselves?
What were the best parts or the worst?
What would be your ideal birthday party?

You will find it useful to make a collection of items connected with birthday parties. These will help you with your project. For example:
- Birthday cards and wrapping paper
- Invitations to parties
- Decorations such as banners, balloons and posters
- Pictures of birthday cakes
- Table decorations such as paper plates and cups
- Birthday menus
- Things to wear such as hats, badges and stickers
- Books about organising parties
- Ideas for party games and activities
- Party recipe books
- Commemorative items such as a 21st birthday key or special cups and mugs.

**Founder's Day at Chelsea Hospital**

**Gravestones**

**Queen Victoria Memorial**

# COMMEMORATION

Commemoration is about keeping the memory of something alive. It often involves a ceremony or celebration of some kind.

### Founder's Day

Many schools, colleges, hospitals and other institutions celebrate Founder's Day: the day when the person responsible for providing the money, the building or starting the work of the institution is remembered. A Founder's Day celebration might take place at your school. There might also be a portrait or statue of the founder of your school displayed in a prominent position.

Find out how your school came to be built; whether a particular person was responsible, when it was first opened and by whom. Find out about the origins of the school name. Is it named after someone or does it come from another source?

### Oakapple Day

The Royal Hospital at Chelsea was founded by Charles II. It provides a home for old soldiers known as Chelsea Pensioners. Founder's Day at the hospital is celebrated on the 29th of May, King Charles II's birthday, which is also known as Oakapple Day because it commemorates the day the King escaped from his enemies by hiding in an oak tree. The pensioners celebrate the day with a parade and inspection, and wear sprigs of oak leaves on their uniforms. They also decorate the statue of King Charles at the hospital with oak leaves.

Symbols of commemoration

*Monuments, memorials, tombs, statues, inscriptions, obelisks, trophies, plaques, gravestones, windows, murals, plates, wreaths.*

**Sir Robert Cotton Memorial Plaque**

**Guy Fawkes Celebrations**

# PEOPLE, their lives, works and beliefs

**If the people mentioned on this page could see how their lives and work are commemorated today, how do you think they might feel? Proud? Important? Clever? Embarrassed? Humble? Brave? Honoured?**

**Alfred Nobel** invented dynamite, and then spent most of his life experimenting with explosives to find ways of making it safe to handle. He always said that it should only be used for peaceful jobs, but governments quickly saw the war potential of a powerful explosive. When he died in 1896 he left a will stipulating that his wealth should form a fund to be distributed annually in the form of five prizes to people whose work had been for the greater benefit of mankind. The Nobel Peace Prize has been awarded every year since 1901.

In a plot to kill King James I by blowing up the Houses of Parliament, barrels of gunpowder were placed in the cellars and **Guy Fawkes** lit the fuse. The plot was betrayed, the building searched, and Guy Fawkes arrested. He wasn't burned on a bonfire but tortured until he had given the names of his fellow conspirators, who were then arrested, hung, drawn and quartered. When people heard the King had been saved they lit bonfires to celebrate. This has been done ever since, putting Guy Fawkes on the top, accompanied by spectacular firework displays.

**Burn's Night**, celebrated by Scots on the 25th of January, commemorates the life and work of the poet Robert Burns. Recitals of his poems, the playing of bagpipes, dancing and the 'piping in the haggis' ceremony mark the occasion.

Imagine you were to attend these events – what might you experience?

**Think about:**
- The sounds you might hear
- The food you might eat
- The clothes you might wear
- The things you might do.

Can you think of other people, still living or not, whose lives should be commemorated? Perhaps explorers, inventors, film stars, pop stars, famous composers, politicians and sports personalities might be on your list. What would be the best way to commemorate them?

# Keeping the past —

**Museums, rallies, re-enactments, restorations, displays, exhibitions and demonstrations are some ways of keeping the past alive.**

Special edition stamps have long commemorated important events and people known for notable achievements. First day covers are of special interest to stamp collectors. If you were responsible for special editions, what would your stamps commemorate?

### Gallantry
*Issue date — 11th September 1990*

Commemorative events may be solemn occasions, with perhaps a religious element. Others are lighthearted but based on historical facts. Some are public occasions, such as rallies and exhibitions, while others can take place in the home.

Things people do to commemorate the lives and works of others:

- Send cards or give flowers
- Write an obituary
- Write a poem or compose special music
- Hold a memorial service
- Perform the work of the person being remembered
- Create an exhibition
- Re-enact an event or dress in the style of the period
- Build a monument, engrave a plaque, or organise an unveiling ceremony
- Renovate something old to preserve it
- Hold a rally
- Stage a carnival or organise a party
- Light fireworks
- Produce special food
- Make souvenirs.

# ALIVE

**How Scotland publicised the 100th birthday of the building of the Forth Rail Bridge in 1990.**

Scotland's most magnificent attraction is the Forth Rail Bridge, which was opened by the Prince of Wales in March 1890.

Known as the 'Eighth Wonder of the World', this mile-long masterpiece of Victorian engineering majestically spans the Firth of Forth just eight miles from Edinburgh, attracting thousands of visitors each year.

This year, Scotland celebrates the Centennial of the Forth Bridge with a huge birthday party that lasts for six months and features one hundred different events. Everyone will be invited to join in the celebrations which will appeal to all ages. Summer highlights include a Regatta, a Jazz Festival, a Race Day and a fabulous Charity Ball. There will be steam train excursions, and a variety of engineering conferences. And on the 7th of October the amazing Birthday Spectacular will light up the Forth Bridge in a breathtaking symphony of fireworks, special effects and water tableaux.

Think about a new commemorative celebration. For example the opening of a new swimming pool, bridge or by-pass, the anniversary of a building or the first landing on the moon. What would you choose to commemorate?

# CARNIVAL

IMAGINE a huge, noisy, colourful procession moving slowly through the streets day and night with music, dancing and exotic costumes. Each year the Rio Carnival in Brazil and the Notting Hill Carnival in London attract thousands of spectators and revellers. An atmosphere of intense excitement is generated which lasts for several days.

**Imagine being a spectator at a large carnival.** Close your eyes, try and think what it would be like. Picture yourself joining in the fun. What would you do? What might it sound like? The music, the bands. Perhaps the crowd is moving. What might it smell like? Discuss your thoughts with others in your group.

**Now think about the differences** between the large event and a smaller village carnival. Compare the two and discuss. Make detailed notes.

**Think about** the information people will need to know about the carnival. Can you add to this list: Name? Date? Time? Location? Route? Is a poster the best means of telling people? What about advertisements in newspapers or magazines, or on television or radio? The carnival route needs very careful planning so that disruption can be minimised and the carnival seen to best effect. What is the best possible way to take into account the size of the carnival, the disruption to traffic and those living or working on the route? Discuss how the carnival might affect local traders and residents.

The spangled and showy costumes of paraders on foot or on floats glitter and shine as they dance to the pulsating music. After dark the party continues, the floats and even some costumes are brightly lit. The carnival procession shimmers and sparkles throughout the night.

Village carnivals involve fewer people. A procession may be decorative and colourful, celebrating local customs and traditions.

Sometimes a fête is also held to raise money for something the village needs, such as church restoration or a new village hall. These could be game stalls and various items for sale. Sometimes school carnivals celebrate school events.

# A Spectacular way to celebrate

A team of people each with their own area of responsibility contributes to the organisation of the carnival: Publicity, Community Relations, Commercial Enterprise Accountant, Parade and Route Manager, Costume and Float Organiser, Public Services Liaison Officer.

**Organising a whole carnival is** usually too much for one person to manage single-handed.

Date? Time?
Location? (Street or school grounds?)
Budget?
Price controls?
How many people might come?
How long will it last?
What is the carnival theme?
Publicity?
Souvenir sellers?
Costumes – who will make them?
Crowd control – barriers?
How many people on foot?
How many floats?
The route?
How will the carnival affect the people who live nearby?
Public transport?
Parking?
Toilets? Food? Picnic areas?
Rubbish disposal?
Security?
Safety – Fire? Police? Ambulance?

**Suppose you had the chance to create** a grand school carnival at the end of the summer term.

- What would it be like?
- What would you celebrate?
- Write down everyone's ideas and group the suggestions into categories, for example, costumes, floats, route, food, public services.
- What conclusions can you draw from these comments?
- Make a list of headings, include categories like time management, publicity, health and safety and contingency plans.

## Listening to others' experiences can help you to identify key considerations

- It was a silly idea for the band to march straight behind the horses!
- It took nine hours to do it instead of the four we planned.
- The ambulance took 20 minutes to get through the crowd.
- I was starving and frozen stiff, the food was hot but twice the price you'd normally pay.
- The poster said there was a fair – where was it?
- I put my bag down for a second – it went – money, picnic and all!
- By the time we'd found a parking space most of the parade was over!
- The noise was so bad I called the police.
- Everything was fine until it rained and my costume fell away in chunks.
- It was 6 o'clock before we found little Johnny screaming his head off.

A float is a moving platform, perhaps a converted lorry or trailer. It is converted into a kind of stage set within the carnival theme. Floats travel in convoy, carrying their costumed passengers through the crowds. They usually compete with each other to create the most noticeable and brightly coloured float. Passengers may dance or shout to the crowds or form a static display called a tableaux.

Can you identify the materials that the float and costumes in the photograph are made of?

If you are designing a costume for a float, you will want it to make the maximum impact on the crowd when seen from a distance. You may need to think about these questions:

- What materials will be most eye-catching?
- Could you recycle any waste material?
- What kinds of fastenings will there be?
- Can the wearer move or dance?
- Can old clothes be adapted?
- Could you use stage make-up or face-paints? (Pay particular attention to eyes and mouth.)
- Can you use existing footwear and change colours, shape and add decoration?
- Do you need to include a head-dress, a mask or a wig?

23

# *Religious* FESTIVALS

A festival is a feast day, a celebration, a time for merrymaking.

**HARVEST** — Consider how food is decorated and presented for all these festivals or how crops are often used to make symbolic objects like the corn dolly.

**CHRISTMAS** — Many religions have traditions associated with light, for example, candles in churches, stained glass windows, or Christmas tree lights.

**EASTER** — The tradition of hot cross buns originated long before Christianity. In pagan times the bun represented the moon and the cross divided it into four quarters. For Christians the cross is a reminder of Jesus' crucifixion on Good Friday.

'Festival' comes from the verb 'to feast' – food features highly in celebrations. There is also a relationship with the word 'fair' from the latin *feria* (holiday). Holidays were 'holy days' when people did not work because they kept the day for religious observance. All religious festivals serve as annual reminders of stories and events that need to be remembered.

Festivals are public occasions where people are able to share their feelings with others. Long ago there were many feasts and festivals which were highlights in the lives of working people. Many of these have been forgotten and are no longer celebrated.

Make a list and think about what occasion you might like to organise a festival for. Think about new festivals as well as historic ones. Consider also what might be worth celebrating in the future.

Harvest festivals are among the oldest of festivals to be celebrated. In ancient times people would pray to their gods for a good harvest and when the crops had grown say 'thank you' by offering up part of the crop. Today harvest festivals still occur all round the world. In Korea people celebrate Chusok. At harvest time in Britain churches are decorated with different foods.

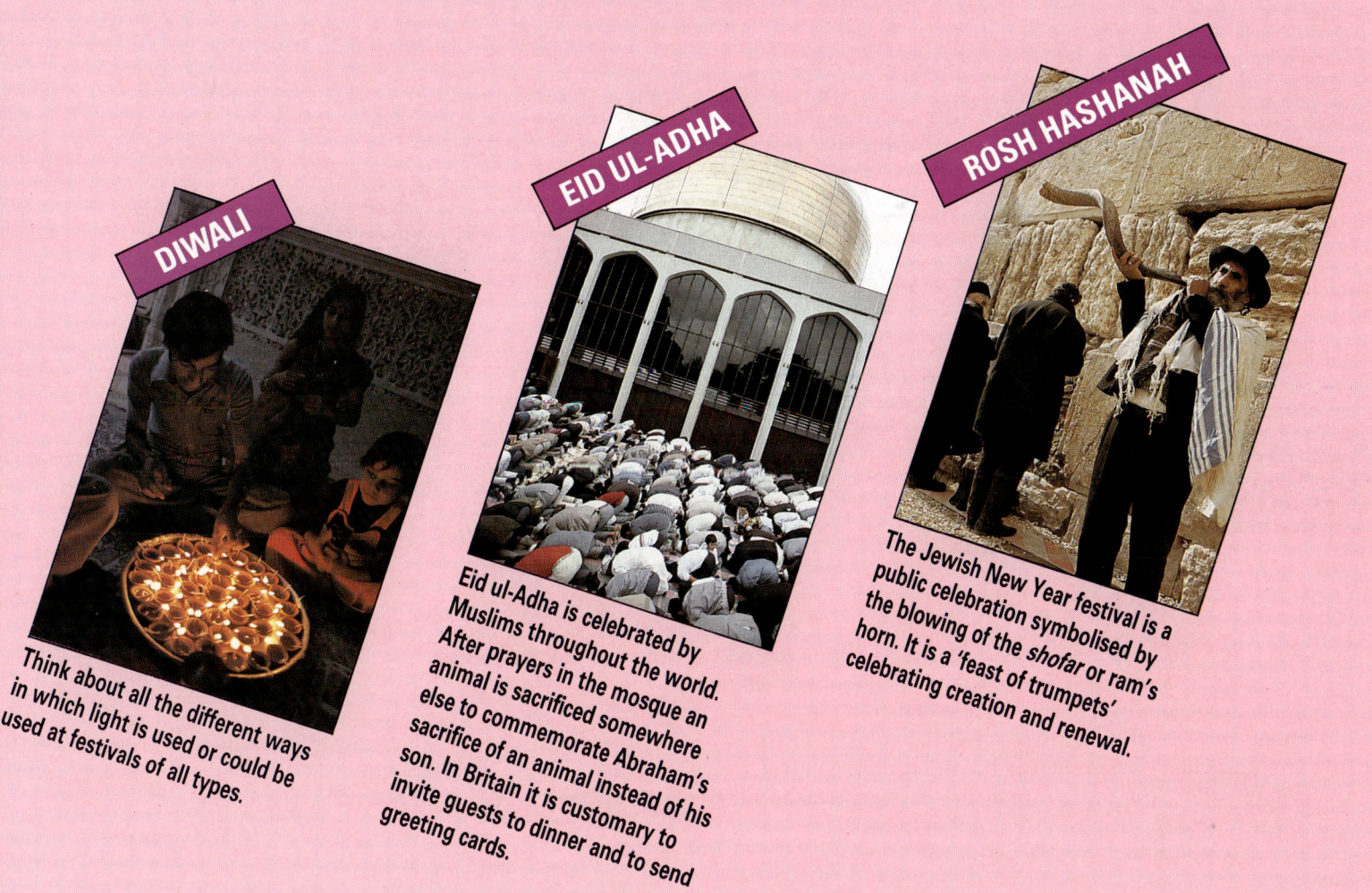

**DIWALI** — Think about all the different ways in which light is used or could be used at festivals of all types.

**EID UL-ADHA** — Eid ul-Adha is celebrated by Muslims throughout the world. After prayers in the mosque an animal is sacrificed somewhere else to commemorate Abraham's sacrifice of an animal instead of his son. In Britain it is customary to invite guests to dinner and to send greeting cards.

**ROSH HASHANAH** — The Jewish New Year festival is a public celebration symbolised by the blowing of the *shofar* or ram's horn. It is a 'feast of trumpets' celebrating creation and renewal.

**Christmas** is one of the most widely celebrated festivals in the world. It is the time when Christians celebrate the birth of Christ, but the rituals we associate with Christmas are much older. They come from the Roman mid-winter festival of Saturnalia a festival in honour of Saturn, god of corn and harvest.

Many other traditions associated with Christmas have a fascinating history of their own. For example, Santa Claus was St. Nicholas, a saintly bishop of Asia Minor.

Traditional Christmas food has changed over time. Christmas pudding was originally a dish called plum porridge which consisted of meat, broth, raisins, currants, prunes, breadcrumbs and spices. As years passed it became thicker and thicker until it became the Christmas pudding we eat today. Mince pies originally contained minced meat.

People celebrate Christmas differently. In Greece there are no Christmas trees or presents; instead, presents are exchanged on St Basil's Day. In Rumania, a special cake (called turte cake) made from layers of dough with melted sugar or honey and crushed walnuts is eaten.

**Diwali** is the Hindu festival of light when people recall the story of Rama and his return after freeing his wife Sita from the demon King Ravana. Throughout India coloured lights are ceremonially lit to decorate homes and streets. Inside homes clay pots contain candles, coloured lights are hung and special lamps lit to welcome Lakshmi, the giver of prosperity. Prayers are offered giving thanks for prosperity in the past and for the future. In Bengal people worship Kali instead of Lakshmi and the festival is called Kali Puja.

**Easter** is a Christian festival celebrating the resurrection of Jesus after his death on the cross.

The name Easter is derived from Eostre, the pagan goddess of spring, who also gave new life to the world and whose festival was held at the Spring Equinox. The Christian festival is tied to these ancient celebrations and Easter eggs continue the custom of eggs representing new life.

# TRADITIONAL FESTIVALS

**THINK ABOUT** those features which many festivals share and those which make them different and distinctive.

Many new festivals have been introduced during recent years. Some celebrate the lives of famous people such as the Dickens Festival, the Burns Festival and Shakespeare's Birthday Festival. Others are associated with particular places such as the Edinburgh Festival, Cheltenham Literature Festival, the Bath Festival and the music festival at Knebworth. Many of these have now become a tradition and are held every year.

Many festivals include:

- Exhibitions
- Films
- Talks
- Puppet shows
- Fireworks
- Opera
- Walks
- Music
- Fun Run
- Recitals
- Dance
- Drama
- Fairs
- Food
- Processions
- Religions
- Lights
- Dressing up
- Comedy.

## NEW YEAR FESTIVALS

**In some parts of Britain** the ancient custom of lighting a fire to celebrate New Year still continues. In Scotland, New Year's Eve, or Hogmanay, is celebrated more than Christmas.

**In Japan**, New Year is called Osyogatsu and is the most important holiday of the year. It is a family festival and there are many special foods and decorations, some of which symbolise good health, happiness and good fortune.

**The Chinese New Year**, Yuan Tan, begins on the first day of the first month of the lunar calendar. It lasts up to 15 days and includes many traditions, special foods, giving of presents to children, colourful processions, music and dancing. The Year of the Dragon, which occurs every twelfth year, is a particularly special occasion. The festivities are deeply religious and end with the lantern festival on the first full moon of the year.

**The Islamic calendar** is based on 12 lunar months beginning with the new moon. This means that the New Year is celebrated 11 or 12 days earlier each year.

**Mid-April marks the beginning of the Bikrami Year** and is an important festival for Sikhs marking the beginning of harvest and the summer.

Some festivals are held annually, others are not
Some festivals cost money to attend, others do not
Some festivals are for people with very specialist interests, others are not
Some festivals are held at the same time each year, others are not
Some festivals are held in the same place each time, others are not

One of the best known modern festivals is the Edinburgh International Festival of Music and Drama. First held in 1947 it runs for three weeks and includes performances of many kinds including orchestral concerts, opera, dance, recitals and drama. At the same time there is an international film festival, a television festival, various exhibitions and a military tattoo.

A Fringe festival, quite separate from the main event, runs alongside the programme and offers 400 events.

**People from various cultures or religions** have different kinds of festivals. Find out about the different traditions and customs. Ask about:

- The kinds of food people eat
- The way people dress
- The history of the festival
- Where and when it takes place
- Whether the festival takes place in a special place or building
- Particular ceremonies during the festival
- Whether it is a public or private occasion
- Whether any rituals are performed
- The emotions people feel and express
- Whether it is a religious occasion
- What kinds of ceremonial objects are used
- What the objects look like.

**Most festivals have a particular theme** and celebrate important occasions. Imagine that you were planning a school festival.
- What might the occasion be?
- What would be on your list of activities?
- How would you attract the maximum number of people?

# Events

EPSOM DERBY

CHELSEA FLOWER SHOW

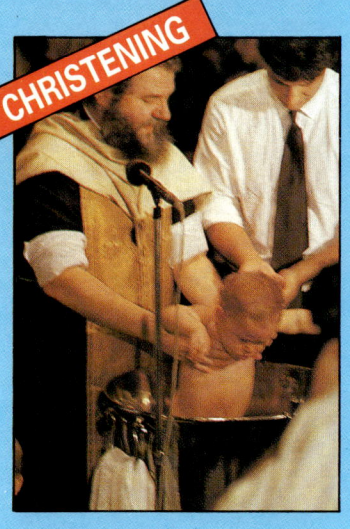

CHRISTENING

WEDDING

EXHIBITION

MOTOR SHOW

AIR DISPLAY

REGATTA

FASHION SHOW

AGRICULTURAL SHOW

Often, events are organised to make a profit – sell more cars, raise funds for a new village hall or to promote a new shop. Others are only concerned with bringing people together to share a special occasion, such as a wedding, a retirement or a home-coming. Sometimes events enable people to demonstrate and be rewarded for skills in a range of activities from breeding and training animals, growing plants and arranging flowers to making things from clocks to cakes.

Events are often organised to celebrate some kind of achievement or milestone. For example, the launch of a new boat, film or shop, or the recognition of personal endeavour such as passing an exam or winning in sport. Some mark an important occasion such as a centenary celebration of a school or company. Many events have become a tradition such as village fêtes, air shows, film and TV awards.

As you look at the examples on this page think about the reasons why they take place. Consider ways they might be categorised, for example, to earn an income, to raise money for a charity, or to share an important occasion with family and friends.

Acknowledgements

The authors and publishers are grateful to the following for permission to reproduce photographs and real items: *Airpic*, Aerial view Nottingham (pp. 4–5); *Bridgeman Art Library*, Bruegel's Peasant Wedding (p. 6); *Bubbles Photo Library*, Group Discussion/J. Woodcock (p. 22); *Celtic Picture Agency*, National Eisteddfod (pp. 3, 18); *Collections* (Brian Shuel), Warrington Walking Day (p. 5), Thamesday Clown (p. 15), Street Party (p. 14), Founder's Day at Chelsea Hospital (pp. 3, 16), Guy Fawkes (p. 17), Hot Cross Buns (p. 24), Chinese New Year (pp. 3, 26), (Anthea Sieveking) Birthday Party (p. 12); D.C. *Thompson and Company*, Forth Bridge Celebrations (pp. 18–19); *Elphick Designs, Faversham*, Badge (p. 12); *Heriot's Catering*, Wedding Cake (pp. 3, 6), Feast (p. 7), Catering Company (p. 7); *Hutchison Library*, Diwali (pp. 2, 25); *Katz Pictures Ltd*, Chelsea Flower Show (pp. 10–11), Epsom Derby/Andrew North (p. 28); *M and G Gray*, Party Invitation (p. 12); *MacDonald's*, Children's Party (p. 13); *Mary Rose Trust*, Mary Rose Restoration (p. 19); *National Motor Museum*, Traction Engine (p. 19); *Post Office*, Stamps (p. 18); *Robert Harding Picture Library*, Candlelit Dinner (p. 6), Morris Dancers (pp. 2, 8), Children in Fancy Dress (p. 8), Boy with Painted Face (p. 8), Headdress (p. 9), Rushbearing Ceremony (p. 21), Harvest Festival (p. 24), Car Show (p. 29), Wedding Couple in Car (p. 28), Chelsea Flower Show (p. 28), Horse and Cattle Parade (p. 29); *Sally and Richard Greenhill*, Snack Stall (p. 6), Gravestones (p. 16), Sir Robert Cotton Plaque (p. 17), Queen Victoria Memorial (p. 16), Notting Hill Carnival (pp. 2, 21), Christian Float (p. 21), Christmas Meal (pp. 3, 26); *Screen Ventures*, Eid Prayers (p. 25); *Second Nature, London*, Pop-up card (p. 12); *Spectrum Colour Library*, Edinburgh Tattoo (p. 27); *York Archaeological Trust*, Jorvik Museum (p. 19); *Zefa Picture Library*, Man with Headdress (p. 9), Birthday Party/J. Feingersh (pp. 3, 15), Boy in Jeans and Cap/Norman (p.13), Houses Float, Rio (p. 23), Valentine Float, Rio (pp. 2, 20–21), Rosh haShanah/ W. Braun (p. 25); Jet Fighters (p. 29), Slava Zeitzev Fashion Show (p. 29), Christening (p. 28), Chagall Museum (p. 28), Henley Royal Regatta (p. 29).

The Nottingham street map is drawn with the permission of the *Nottingham City Council*.

Every effort has been made to contact copyright holders and we apologise if any have been overlooked.